The Wildlife of Yellowstone

Written by Todd Crawford

Illustrated by Rachel Feirman

Yellowstone became the very first national park in the United States in 1872.
The park is located mostly in Wyoming, with some parts in Montana and Idaho.

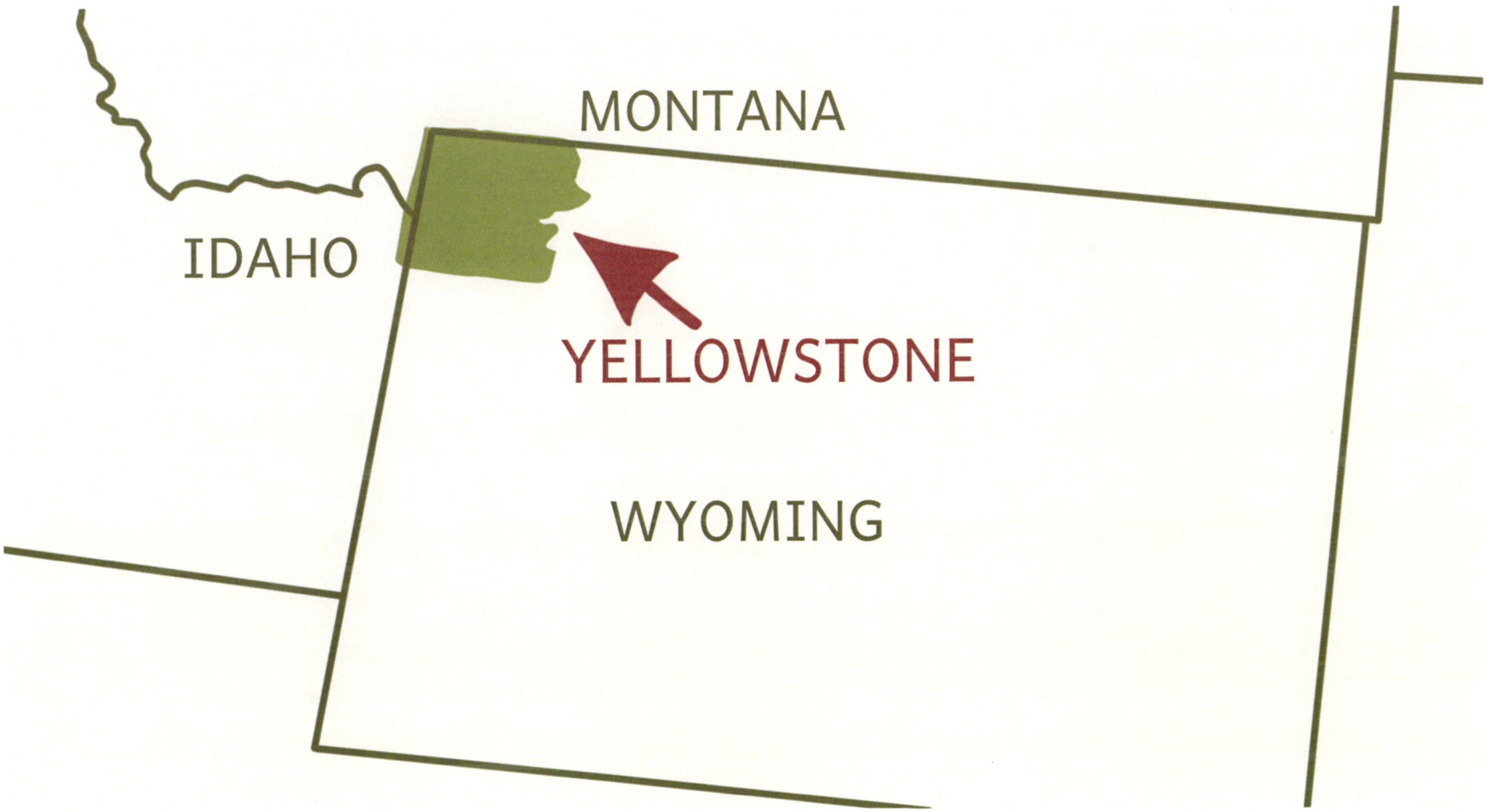

Yellowstone National Park Rules

In the great outdoors, you should never approach any wild animal.
Stay 25 yards away from large animals like elk, deer, moose and bison.
If you see a bear or a wolf, stay 100 yards away.
That is as far as eight school busses lined up!

Be Safe!

Bison, elk, and all other animals
25 yards

Bears and wolves
100 yards

Yellowstone National Park is home to 200 different species or kinds of animals.

Discover and learn about many of the animals in the park while reading this book and look for smaller animals within each illustration. Find them all!

Badgers are plentiful in Yellowstone, but are very hard to see because they are mostly active at night. They measure about two feet long and weigh about 20 pounds. Badgers are major predators that eat squirrels, gophers and other small rodents. They also eat birds and eggs. Mountain lions, bears and wolves prey on badgers. They can live up to 14 years!

Common Ravens are large black birds about two feet long. They eat almost anything, sometimes following wolf packs, waiting to feed on their kills. Ravens are extremely smart. They can mimic other bird calls and they have even been seen unzipping backpacks. They can live up to 20 years.

Bison are the largest mammals in North America. They are as big as a car! There are about 5000 bison in Yellowstone that can be seen roaming the valleys. Bison are social animals and like to be around others. They are often seen eating grasses while in herds. They are fast too, running up to 30 miles per hour! Bison can live up to 20 years.

Do not approach a bison while in the park!

The Grizzly Bear is the largest predator in Yellowstone. Grizzly bears are omnivores. They kill for meat and fish, but also eat grass, insects and berries. There are about 730 grizzly bears living in the park. Grizzlies are very large bears standing as high as eight feet tall! They are really fast and can run up to 40 miles per hour. They hibernate or sleep in dens during the winter months. A grizzly bear can live up to 30 years.

Do not approach any bear while in the park!

The Cougar or mountain lion is the largest cat in North America. There are only about 40 cougars living in the park, so it is very rare to see one! They can weigh as much as 170 pounds. Cougars prey on elk calves and mule deer. They also eat smaller rodents like the marmot. Cougars live between 8-14 years.

Coyotes are abundant in Yellowstone. They can be seen in meadows and fields. They are often mistaken for wolves. Coyotes are smaller, measuring about 18 inches tall at their shoulders and weigh between 25-35 pounds. They mostly eat rodents and rabbits. They are called “song dogs” because of the way they howl to communicate with other coyotes. Coyotes can live between 6-13 years.

The River Otter is sleek and has thick fur perfect for all seasons in Yellowstone. They are the best swimmers in the weasel family. They grow to be about 50 inches long and weigh between 10-30 pounds. When underwater their ears and nose close. They can hold their breath for up to two to three minutes at a time. River otters eat fish, turtles, frogs and crayfish. Otters often live to be 12 years.

Black Bears are very common in Yellowstone and can be seen quite often. When cars are stopped to watch bears, it is called a bear jam! Do not get out of your car! Black bears can weigh up to 300 pounds! They are almost three feet tall while on all fours. While standing, they may reach as high as five to seven feet tall. They are excellent tree climbers. Black bears eat rodents, insects, fish, elk calves and some vegetation. They can live up to 30 years!

Stay at least 100 yards away from any bear in Yellowstone.

Wolves are a very important part of Yellowstone's history. There are only about 100 wolves in Yellowstone. They can be as tall as three feet at the shoulders and can measure up to six feet from nose to tail. A wolf can weigh up to 130 pounds. They roam in small packs with about 10 wolves to a pack. Wolves feed mostly on elk, but also eat bison, deer and some vegetation. Wolves live between four to five years.

Stay at least 100 yards away from wolves in the park!

The Cutthroat Trout is the most abundant kind of trout in Yellowstone. They have red, pink or orange lines on their jaws, which gives them the cutthroat name. They measure between 6-20 inches long. Trout eat insects, smaller fish and sometimes frogs! Cutthroat trout live in cold streams and lakes. They provide food for many different animals in the park. They can live up to 11 years!

Bats are amazing mammals. They are the only mammal that can fly! There are 13 bat species located in Yellowstone. Bats are highly social creatures living together in caves and buildings in the park. They can be seen in the early morning and evenings flying around catching insects. A bat can eat as many as 4000 mosquitos in one night! Bats hibernate in the winter months. They can live between seven and 30 years!

Moose are very large deer. They can stand almost eight feet tall! Bulls or males can have an antler rack as wide as five feet! Around 200 moose live in Yellowstone along lakes and waterways. Moose live alone or in small groups. They eat water plants, twigs and leaves of the willow tree. Moose can live up to 20 years.

Stay at least 25 yards away from a moose!

The Wolverine is an elusive carnivore belonging to the weasel family. There are not many wolverines in the park, so seeing one would be incredible! They are generally around 40 inches long and can weigh up to 30 pounds. They eat small rodents, eggs, squirrels, mice and birds. They can live up to 13 years.

Elk are the most plentiful large mammal living in the park. As many as 20,000 of them can be seen spread out in seven different herds. Male elk are very large with their antlers growing as wide as an adult is tall! Elk like to eat grasses and the bark of aspen trees. They can live up to 18 years old. Bull elk are the most photographed animal in the park, but can also be aggressive towards people.

Stay at least 25 yards away from elk.

www.ingramcontent.com/pod-product-compliance
Ingram Content Group UK Ltd.
Pitfield, Milton Keynes, MK11 3LW, UK
UKRC031108040826
14089UKWH00041B/256

9798218179342

9 798218 179342